Introduction

Winterthur Today

Visitors approach Winterthur along a winding road that draws them into a rural landscape of rolling meadows, stone bridges, and distant barns. Beyond lie 200 acres of a naturalistic landscape garden which is intersected by paths that invite exploration and lead ultimately to the museum. A large building whose size is masked by its secure placement on a hillside, the museum houses the world's foremost collection of American decorative arts.

There are many links between the garden and the museum: both provide countless opportunities for quiet contemplation and visual stimulation; both follow the same design principles with an emphasis on color, balance, and proportion; both feature collections that represent the highest quality – plants in the garden and antiques in the museum. Taken together, they offer visitors a rare opportunity to experience the feeling of being in a world set apart, one where there is time for leisurely walks and thoughtful encounters with the American past.

While the garden and the museum form the public face of Winterthur, there is much more to be found there. Winterthur is also a research library containing more than 500,000 books, manuscripts, drawings, prints, photographs, and other printed material; a center for advanced study in American material culture and art conservation; and a series of shops that sell reproductions from Winterthur's collection, plants grown on the estate, and a wide range of gifts. In addition, Winterthur is the former home of Henry Francis du Pont, a scion of the family whose industrial achievement has an important place in American history and the man most responsible for assembling the decorative arts collection and creating the garden.

Winterthur is perhaps best known for its decorative arts collection, a dazzling array of more than 89,000 objects including furniture, textiles, ceramics, silver and other metals, architectural elements, tools, needlework, prints, and paintings. No other collection of American antiques approaches the quality, variety, and depth represented at Winterthur. The focus is on the finest examples of American craftsmanship made between 1640 and 1860. The scope is wide – high-style, vernacular, and ethnic objects are represented. Viewed together or individually, these objects evoke the talents, visions, and aspirations from over 200 years of American life.

Visitors to the museum see these objects presented in almost 200 period room settings and display areas. Most rooms are without barriers, and all visitors have a unique opportunity of experiencing the collection firsthand. A schoolgirl's careful stitches in a sampler, the silversmith's hammer marks on a tankard, and the joiner's compass marks on a seventeenth-century painted chest are readily visible and allow personal involvement with the objects.

What can be learned from this involvement with objects? How does looking at a piece of porcelain, a Queen Anne card table, or an appliquéd quilt enhance one's understanding of the American past? Every object, old or new, is the result of choice: choices made by the craftsman who created it, the patron who purchased it, the family who preserved it, and in the case of an old object, the collector who acquired it. Thinking about choices – why they were made and who made them – leads to greater understanding, not only of the objects but also of the people who interacted with them.

Helping visitors to learn to look at objects and think about their meaning is the role of the guide. Since its opening in 1951, the museum has emphasized personal interpretation. The subject matter explored between guide and visitor is rich and varied. The interaction may begin with identification of objects, but it moves on to discuss the relationship of one object to another and of the past to the present.

The Winterthur landscape is a natural extension of the museum and functions as an essential context for it. The common threads of design, style, and color link the museum and the garden as do careful attention to detail and concern for harmony. Each complements and reinforces the other, providing visitors with a uniquely satisfying experience.

Winterthur is a garden for all seasons. In winter the immense size of the trees becomes evident as they are silhouetted against a snow-covered field or a gray sky. Spring arrives early, however, and the winter landscape is softened by thousands of snowdrops, aconites, and glory-of-the-snows. Early March brings Chinese witch-hazels, squills, and crocuses. Glorious color appears in April with early rhododendrons and magnolias and reaches a crescendo in May when the full bloom in Azalea Woods transforms the landscape into something akin to an Impressionist painting. Summer is a time of serenity. The color green – in many shades and textures – predominates and cools the landscape, while man-made ponds, fed by Clenny Run, provide restful interludes throughout the garden. Autumn brings a return of color as the leaves turn, berries abound, and colchicums cover Oak Hill.

At any season the garden invites exploration and entertainment. Plant labels, maps, bloom lists, and other interpretive material aid visitors who wish to walk in the garden. During every season except winter, a tram tour is available, narrated by guides who discuss the development of the garden over time, the philosophy that directed its creation, as well as the individual plants and specimens. And at all seasons, special events and programs are offered in the garden.

History of Winterthur

As early as 1810, the land comprising the original Winterthur estate was owned by the du Pont family. Initially purchased by Eleuthère Irénée du Pont, founder of the company's black-powder mills on the banks of Brandywine Creek, the land was acquired by Jacques Antoine Bidermann in 1837. Bidermann was du Pont's chief business associate and son-in-law, who married Evelina Gabrielle du Pont in 1816. When Bidermann retired from the company in 1837, he and Evelina moved to their new property, located a few miles from the powder works. They named the estate Winterthur after the city of Winterthur, Switzerland, ancestral home of the Bidermann family. There they built a house in the popular Greek-revival style and settled down to a life devoted to their farm and gardens.

Scientific farming and a passion for gardening were traits shared by many members of the du Pont family. During their years at Winterthur, the Bidermanns laid the foundations for these activities which were enthusiastically carried out by the next owner of the estate, Colonel Henry Algernon du Pont, the Bidermann's nephew. The colonel was a man of many roles. He served with distinction in the Civil War and had a successful career in the military. Following his retirement from the army, he entered the business world, working both for Du Pont Company and the Wilmington and Northern Railroad, of which he became president. From 1906 until 1917 he represented Delaware as a United States senator.

The colonel and his wife, Mary Pauline Foster du Pont, encouraged their children, Henry Francis and Louise, to explore the woods, meadows, and farmlands of their home and to appreciate its natural beauty. As a young man, Henry Francis studied practical horticulture at Harvard's Bussey Institution. Following his return to Winterthur in 1902, he worked with his father to establish the agricultural landscape and develop the garden that remain the hallmarks of Winterthur. He also embarked on a series of landscape design experiments and color studies that formed the basis for the naturalistic approach and imaginative color combinations evident in the garden today.

In 1914 the colonel turned the management of the Winterthur farms over to his son and, with him, laid out the Pinetum, a collection of coniferous trees that still forms an especially intriguing area of the garden. The colonel also remodeled and enlarged the house several times, culminating in a large addition in 1902 that included a new wing across the front of the original house.

Henry Francis du Pont inherited Winterthur on his father's death in 1926. He continued and greatly expanded the colonel's work in the garden and farm. But it was his own personal interest in collecting American antiques that led him to build another extensive addition to the house between 1929 and 1931.

Du Pont began buying American antiques because he believed that "the early-American arts and crafts had not been given the recognition they deserved," and so he assembled "examples of architecture, furniture and widely divergent early-American materials of all kinds . . . that would show America as it had been."

To create period rooms, du Pont installed antique architectural elements in the Winterthur house. In each of these settings, he placed the objects that best complemented the architecture. Delicately inlaid furniture of the federal period matches equally delicate plaster composition ornament in the Baltimore Drawing Room; the elaborate carving on Philadelphia Chippendale chairs echoes the carving on the woodwork from a 1764 Philadelphia town house; paneled chests

and walls stand together in a seventeenth-century room.

Each display area underwent countless changes and experiments as du Pont sought just the right blend of furniture, ceramics, textiles, metals, and paintings. Much as an artist paints a picture, he used the architecture as a canvas and mixed color, textures, and design to achieve an aesthetically pleasing composition.

The period room settings seen at Winterthur today represent not only du Pont's original work but also the work of a succeeding generation of directors and curators. As research goes on in the field of American decorative arts and material life, the collection is constantly refined and reshaped to reflect current scholarship. Thus the arrangement of objects continues to change as old evidence is challenged and new discoveries are made.

At the same time that he was enlarging the house, du Pont commissioned a long-time friend, Marian Cruger Coffin, to serve as landscape architect for the expansion of the garden. Coffin designed a classically proportioned flight of steps leading to a swimming pool (now the Reflecting Pool), two stone bathhouses, flower beds, and a naturalistic glade and pool for the eastern side of the new addition. On the western side of the house, the gracefully curving roads, stone steps, and bridges are characteristic of her work.

Henry Francis du Pont's passion for Americana and plants continued unabated, culminating in the late 1940s with his decision to turn Winterthur into a museum and a garden for "the education and enjoyment of the American public." Winterthur opened to the public in October 1951 and has since attracted hundreds of thousands of visitors who come to view the very best in early American craftsmanship and a highly articulated vision of the American landscape.

Throughout the ensuing years, the interior of the house and the garden have continued to change and grow. In 1957 Coffin and du Pont collaborated on the Sundial Garden, a collection of April-flowering small trees and shrubs. It was the first area at Winterthur created specifically for the public. Two years later another wing was built at the south end of the museum. Interiors were added or altered as research in American decorative arts, much of it conducted at Winterthur, revealed new directions in scholarship. In 1969 another major addition, the Louise du Pont Crowninshield Research Building, was joined to the museum by a glass-enclosed corridor. Named for Henry Francis du Pont's sister, the building houses the library and conservation facilities.

Although du Pont lessened his involvement in the collection once his home had become a museum, he always remained the "head gardener." Between 1960 and his death at age eighty-nine in 1969, he continued to create new areas and refine those begun years before. Restoring and maintaining du Pont's original design intent is an ongoing activity.

Other Aspects of Winterthur

As a center for the advanced study of early American culture, Winterthur attracts scholars and graduate students who come to study the collection and use the resources of the library. Each year ten graduate students enter the Winterthur Program in Early American Culture, a two-year master's degree program administered jointly with the University of Delaware, which provides training for careers as curators, educators, and arts administrators. Many students go on to pursue a doctorate in American civilization. The Art Conservation Program is another cooperative endeavor with the University of Delaware. It offers a three-year curriculum in all aspects of art conservation leading to a master of science degree. Established scholars are offered one- to six-month fellowships annually for study

in residence. Winterthur also sponsors an annual scholarly conference that addresses topics of current interest in the field of American material culture. A publications program makes the fruits of this research available to a larger public through books, conference proceedings, and the periodical *Winterthur Portfolio: A Journal of American Material Culture*.

Winterthur is actively involved in the surrounding community. Throughout the year the grounds are opened for events such as steeplechase races, elaborate picnics, Easter-egg hunts, footraces, and concerts. There is also a Winterthur away from Winterthur: located 20 miles south of the estate is Odessa, an eighteenth-century grain-shipping port which retains many examples of eighteenth- and nineteenth-century architecture. Winterthur owns and administers the Historic Houses of Odessa: the Corbit-Sharp House, the Wilson-Warner House, the Collins-Sharp House, and the Brick Hotel Gallery. In addition to guided tours, they also offer special community events such as craft fairs, handicrafts classes, and seasonal festivals.

Museum, garden, library, conservation laboratories, shops, publications, historic buildings, and community gathering place are some of the many faces of Winterthur. They all help to fulfill the vision of Winterthur that Henry Francis du Pont articulated many years ago:

I sincerely hope that the Museum will be a continuing source of inspiration and education for all time, and that the gardens and grounds will themselves be a country place museum where visitors may enjoy as I have, not only the flowers, trees, and shrubs, but also the sunlit meadows, shady wood paths, and the peace and quiet calm of a country place which has been loved and taken care of for three generations.

Pauline K. Eversmann

Overleaf: Port Royal Parlor

Latimeria Summerhouse in Peony Garden

Wentworth Room

Winterthur Hall

du Pont Dining Room

Hall of Statues

Flowering Dogwood and annual flowers at Reflecting Pool

China Shop

Georgia Dining Room

Red Lion Inn Facade

Kershner Bakehouse

Kershner Kitchen

Rhododendron mucronulatum
'Cornell Pink'
and Sargent Cherry

Chinese export
porcelain garniture

Readbourne Stair Hall

Flock Room

Evergreens on west lawn

Rare English and
American glassware

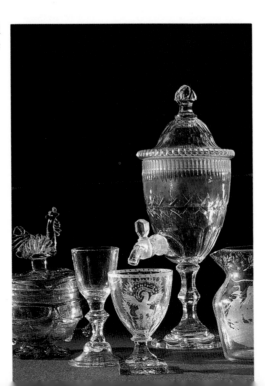

Clocks and watch boxes   Clockmaking tools from the Dominy family   *Overleaf:* Chinese Parlor

Kershner Parlor

Early spring landscape
with cherry trees

North end of museum
from the March Bank

Cecil Bedroom

Oyster Bay Room

Daffodils in April

Lower Pond from Oak Hill

Blackwell Parlor

Carved detail from a 17th-century chest

Dominy Woodworking Shop

Canada geese in Winterthur's rural landscape

Shaker Dwelling Room

Shaker boxes

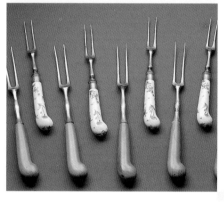

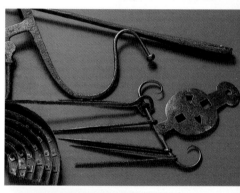

A montage of objects
from the rich collections
of Winterthur's
museum and library.

Vauxhall Room

Hart Room

Previous page: Poéticus Daffodils
on Clenny Run

Red Lion Inn Entrance Hall

Children's toys on display during
Yuletide at Winterthur

End Shop on Shop Lane

Azaleas along Clenny Run   Patuxent Room   *Overleaf:* Readbourne Parlor

Baltimore Room   Ancient Tulip-poplars in winter

Sweeps of azaleas on Oak Hill

Chinese export porcelain

Dining Room Cross Hall   *Overleaf:* Pennsylvania Folk Art Room

Children's furnishings on a quilt

A medley of baskets

Fraktur Room

Silver tea service in the Baltimore Drawing Room

Empire Parlor

Williams Room

Montmorenci Stair Hall

Aerial view of Winterthur in autumn

Marlboro Room

Reflecting Pool from East Terrace

Copyright 1991 by the Henry Francis du Pont Winterthur Museum, Inc.
Paper edition ISBN 0-912724-21-8, Cloth edition ISBN 0-912724-22-6
This book, or portions thereof, may not be reproduced
in any manner without the written permission of the
Henry Francis du Pont Winterthur Museum, Winterthur,
Delaware 19735.
Photography by staff and Stephen Brown, Kevin Fleming,
Gottlieb Hampfler, and Robert Lautman
Design by Donald G. Paulhus
Produced for Winterthur by Fort Church Publishers, Inc.,
Little Compton, Rhode Island 02837
Printed in Japan